Contents

Introduction

A company's vitality relies on revenue generated by loyal customers. This necessitates a proficient sales team, making sales managers crucial in many organizations. We will guide you in establishing and overseeing a successful sales team, providing step-by-step insights into recruiting, motivating, deploying, and evaluating sales representatives. Similar to marketing, sales management is an engaging career, requiring talent and commitment. We'll equip you with the skills to excel as a sales manager.

Adapting to the challenges of modern customer service is crucial for continued success in the new economy. To navigate this landscape effectively, consider the changes in customer service, address issues like safety protocols and stock shortages, and handle interactions with assertive customers. Achieving excellence in customer experience despite external factors is key for success in this evolving environment.

To grow your business, you have two options: work tirelessly on various ideas or take a strategic approach by slowing down, defining clear goals, and crafting a strong plan. While both methods may lead to growth, strategic planning ensures faster and more efficient business development, saving time and resources. Strategic planning is often overlooked but is crucial for success in business development. We'll learn the necessity of a strategic approach to business development, involving goal setting, target clarification, and actionable plans for success. Let's avoid the pitfalls and work smarter and more strategically in your business development endeavors.

Acquiring new clients is a resource-intensive process, often overlooked compared to the cost-effective strategy of retaining existing customers. This neglect can lead to complacency, resulting in the loss of valuable relationships. Maintaining client relationships is a low-cost, high-value endeavor. We'll explore essential aspects of post-purchase client management, including relationship selling, personal interactions, automation for seamless communication, and strategies for recovering from setbacks, illustrated practical tips.

In the realm of business, the shift towards online direct-to-consumer (B-to-C) models is driven by the presence of customers on the internet. We'll explore the opportunities and challenges of online B-to-C, emphasizing the importance of reaching customers where they are. Topics include identifying and targeting your real customer, creating relevant content, and utilizing tools like search engine optimization and social media marketing to attract and engage the right audience cost-effectively. As buying behavior remains constant, the focus is on adapting to the changing landscape of where customers make their purchases. Discover why many companies are embracing online direct sales and how you can strategically position yourself to connect with your audience in this evolving digital landscape.

Many sales professionals associate the term "process" with rigid scripts and reports created by individuals unfamiliar with the challenges of meeting sales quotas. Some claim to have a sales process but struggle to articulate its specifics. In contrast, successful salespeople can precisely outline their actions before, during, and after each sales call. This book will comprehensively address the why, what, and how of a highly effective sales process, offering insights to integrate it seamlessly into your routine. You will learn to compete at a global level, cultivating loyal clients who consistently seek your assistance.

Managing a sales organization is challenging—you're leading, managing, and selling. Balancing tasks like forecasting, creating compensation plans, and defining sales territories can be overwhelming. The solution? Sales operations. It's the key to efficient time management, enabling your business to grow and scale while handling essential operational tasks.

Collaboration has been identified as a top-five skill desired by employers across various industries. Proficient teamwork is crucial for career development in fields like healthcare, government, sports, education, technology, and the military. Research indicates that effective teams consistently achieve better outcomes than individuals or poorly coordinated groups. Despite this, many teams struggle to reach their full potential. Achieving optimal team performance relies on exceptional intra-team communication. We'll explore the practices of high-performing teams and highlights the pitfalls of inefficient teams. The concepts presented can be immediately applied to enhance collaborative efforts. You will learn practical strategies to improve communication, collaboration, and overall team output.

Chapter 1 Sales Management

What is sales management?

Sales management is a cyclical process integral to creating and overseeing a sales team. It begins with understanding the overall marketing strategy, which is then translated into a focused sales task. This task outlines the specifics for successful sales, including target customers, products, and sales approaches. Decisions and actions of the sales manager are guided by this task. Recruiting, hiring, training, and motivating skilled salespeople are crucial steps in building an effective team. Structuring territories, setting quotas, and designing a performance-based compensation program are subsequent aspects tailored to the sales task. Measurement and accountability for results are essential, focusing on key metrics linked to the sales task. This data-driven and disciplined approach to sales management ensures success in a competitive landscape and feeds back into the marketing strategy for continuous improvement.

Defining the sales task

Defining the sales task is the crucial first step in sales management, providing the foundation for subsequent activities. To specify the sales task, address four key questions. First, identify the target customers with precision, such as calling on specific purchasing managers in hospitals within defined geographic areas. Second, determine the products and services to be sold, detailing the focus for each team member, like selling diagnostic equipment to cancer centers. Third, outline the specific activities sales reps must undertake during the selling process, including calls, demonstrations, negotiations, and follow-ups. Lastly, establish communication channels for the team to report back to the company, ensuring clarity on where to seek support, whether from customer service, shipping, financing, or other departments. This structured approach enhances efficiency and effectiveness in the sales process.

Recruiting salespeople

Recruiting and hiring sales representatives are crucial tasks that top sales managers actively engage in as an ongoing process. To guide the hiring process, first, create a profile outlining the skills, knowledge, and dispositions required for the sales task. Collaborate with the HR team to develop a job description based on this profile and the duties outlined in the sales task. Potential recruits can come from various sources, including internal employees, referrals, agencies, universities, military personnel, online job platforms, and traditional advertising. Use a focused interview script, employing situation or behavior-based questions that align with the sales task's requirements. Alternatively, conduct performance-based interviews with exercises simulating sales activities.

When you identify the right candidate, extend a fair but strong employment offer, emphasizing their value to the organization.

Conducting sales training

Establishing a formal sales training program is crucial for ensuring the success of your sales team. Begin by deconstructing the sales task into a comprehensive list of specific skills, knowledge, and behaviors required for the job. Unlike the recruiting process, aim for completeness in these lists, considering both existing and needed competencies. For instance, a sales rep for surgical instruments would need skills in call planning, presentations, product demonstrations, securing commitments, and order processing. Knowledge requirements might include human anatomy, surgical procedures, operating room protocols, and surgeon professionalism. Desired behaviors could encompass being self-motivated, professional, organized, engaging, and persuasive.

Develop training modules based on these lists, assigning qualified individuals, such as star sales reps, sales managers, marketing managers, technical teams, or even customers, to deliver the training. Consider role-playing exercises to allow reps to practice skills expected in the field. A well-designed sales training program not only motivates your reps but also demonstrates the company's commitment to their success, ensuring a swift start to building your business.

Motivating salespeople

Motivating salespeople is a challenging aspect of the job, and as a sales manager, it's crucial to address. Motivation is key for creating enthusiasm, reducing turnover, and ensuring productivity and confidence in accomplishing the sales task. Successful sales managers use a mix of intrinsic rewards, such as autonomy, interesting product reminders, and a sense of company loyalty, as well as extrinsic rewards like financial incentives, awards, titles, and recognition. Regular events recognizing successful reps, involving them in training programs and important meetings, and arranging mentoring opportunities or participation in a sales advisory council contribute to their sense of usefulness and importance. Conducting short-term sales contests and emphasizing customer feedback further boost motivation. Inviting winning reps' customers to award events adds a personal touch and reinforces the direct impact of their efforts. Ultimately, keeping talented salespeople motivated is crucial for long-term success.

Defining a sales force structure

Creating a sales structure involves determining the number of sales reps needed and their organization. Two approaches for determining the number of reps are top-down, where total annual revenue goal is divided by average sales per customer, and bottom-up, where the total number of customers is considered. Once the number of reps is established, the next step is to decide on their organization—whether they should be product-focused, customer-focused, or geography-focused. Using a matrix that pairs products with customer types helps define the sales task for each combination. If sales tasks are similar in columns, organizing by product is preferred; if similar in rows, organizing by customer type is suitable. If all sales tasks are the same, organizing reps by geography is recommended.

Forecasting sales performance

Creating territories involves forecasting both market potential and sales potential in your areas. Market potential represents the expected sales for your entire industry in that area, while sales potential is your company's share of that market. Forecasts can be based on objective data, such as historical sales trends, or subjective data, relying on expert opinions from individuals or groups. Two recommended approaches are the top-down and bottom-up methods. The top-down approach starts with assessing the national economic level, industry potential, and estimating your company's share of the industry. In contrast, the bottom-up approach involves each sales rep estimating their territory's overall production, considering factors like customer loyalty and competition. The territory forecasts are then aggregated to determine the company-level sales potential.

Creating sales territories

For creating sales territories, I recommend two approaches: the buildup method and the breakdown method, similar to the forecasting methods of top-down and bottom-up. The buildup method involves starting at the individual rep level, considering their workload capacity and customer visit frequency. Determine the types of customers, products/services, and sales tasks, then set geographical boundaries for each rep based on customer density. The breakdown method, on the other hand, starts with the overall company sales potential and divides it by the number of reps to establish sales expectations for each. Create geographical territories accordingly.

Tips for creating sales territories include using existing geographical boundaries like states, counties, cities, or zip codes, ensuring clarity and preventing interference between reps. Prioritize equalizing sales potential rather than physical size, and align financial and IT systems to track sales within these boundaries. Regularly adapt territory boundaries to accommodate changes in market conditions, rep dynamics, and competition. Well-designed sales territories contribute to customer satisfaction, reduced costs, and motivated, productive reps.

Setting sales quotas

A sales quota is a targeted sales amount that serves as a crucial tool in sales management. It directly aligns sales reps with the company's strategy and sales task, helping allocate resources effectively and, most importantly, serving as a motivating factor. To set quotas, start by collecting data on each territory's potential market sales versus the rep's sales history. Consider territory differences in economic conditions, competition, and travel times. Adjust quotas based on current penetration and individual rep ability, considering factors like growth potential and market share. Not every rep will have the same quota, and adjustments should reflect the difficulty of achieving the quota. Ensure fairness and motivation by communicating clear quotas and explaining the determination process to reps. Quotas signal confidence in the rep's ability to succeed, acting as a contract between the sales manager and the rep. Careful and thoughtful quota setting is essential for supporting the team and achieving desired results.

Understanding sales compensation

To effectively manage a sales force, it's crucial to implement a compensation program that aligns with market standards and encourages desired behaviors in sales reps. The compensation structure can influence the quantity and quality of sales calls, as well as the time devoted to the job, depending on the specific sales task. Designing a successful sales compensation program requires collaboration with departments such as finance and human resources. It should be simple, fair, flexible, affordable, and competitive. Assess the strengths and weaknesses of your current program, ensuring alignment with the company's strategic direction and competitiveness in the market. Seek input from various stakeholders, including senior management, sales teams, and support groups. Evaluate the program's administration efficiency and explore ways to streamline and enhance flexibility. A well-designed sales compensation plan integrates seamlessly with all aspects of sales management, showcasing the effectiveness of a tailored approach for each company.

Designing sales compensation programs

To create a sales compensation program, follow these four steps. First, determine the desired annual earnings for each rep by assessing past performance and making adjustments as needed. Ensure the amount is competitive within the industry. Second, choose the compensation method, such as a straight salary, variable commission, or a combination of both. Variable commission plans directly tie earnings to sales but may carry more risk for reps, making a combination program popular. Third, set thresholds for the variable portion, whether fixed amounts, percentages, or varied payments based on quotas. For instance, consider increasing commission rates after reaching specific sales milestones. Finally, test the program using last year's sales results to evaluate if it aligns with goals, drives desired behaviors, offers sufficient motivation, and maintains a suitable balance between fixed salary and variable commission. A well-designed sales compensation program integrates with various elements of sales management for overall success.

Communicating sales compensation

The best compensation plan can fail without proper communication. Create a formal written document outlining the plan, its industry comparisons, and details on how and when reps earn money, including examples. Coordinate with finance and HR to ensure budget compliance and policy adherence. Conduct verbal presentations, announcing the plan to the sales force and having one-on-one meetings with reps. Address special situations, explaining changes when a rep's compensation may decrease. After communication, administer the plan effectively by providing continuous feedback, clear documentation of earnings calculations, adherence to pay schedules, and prompt resolution of compensation issues. Measure the plan's success against objectives, analyzing metrics such as sales, profits, or market share. Continuously assess plan simplicity and effectiveness, avoiding end-of-year surprises. Proactive monitoring is crucial for successful sales management.

Managing underperforming reps

Sales managers often encounter underperforming reps despite having effective compensation systems. To address this, analyze overall team performance using sales call reports and results. Assess whether reps target the right accounts and activities, and check for customer complaints or signs of issues. Diagnose underperformance by identifying if reps lack the necessary skills or willingness for the sales task. If it's a skills gap, refer to the sales competency model, identify deficiencies, and collaborate with training or HR for a tailored remedial program. Ensure the rep acknowledges the areas needing improvement and commits to closing the gap. If the sales task has changed, review it with the rep and observe their performance in a sales call. Address the challenge when a rep knows the job but doesn't perform due to issues like motivation, pay, or personal problems. Help them overcome the situation while setting clear deadlines for improvement. If deadlines aren't met, consider finding a new rep for the territory. Effective sales management requires individualized attention, recognizing the diverse skills, ambitions, and career paths of each rep.

Measuring sales performance

Sales managers ensure accountability by measuring both outputs and inputs of their team members. Outputs, such as sales revenue and new accounts, are complemented by inputs like the number of calls, days worked, and selling time per call. To effectively gauge performance, analyze ratios of inputs to outputs. For instance, compare the calls per day by evaluating the ratio of sales calls to days worked. Utilizing these ratios, create a sales effectiveness index to assess who achieves the most output relative to their input. Focus on meaningful measurements that impact behavior, communicate evaluation criteria clearly, and continuously measure to facilitate timely corrective actions. Engaging in thoughtful conversations alongside accurate data reinforces the manager's commitment to helping reps succeed.

Creating the virtual sales task

Sales managers must adapt to changes in the marketplace, especially in the current virtual work environment. Updating the sales task playbook involves addressing four key questions. Firstly, reevaluate the target customers in the virtual context, considering expanded access to different customer types. Next, identify products and services, incorporating potential enhancements through virtual technologies. Thirdly, define virtual activities required for sales success, considering efficiency gains and limitations compared to in-person interactions.

Lastly, set guidelines for reaching out to various departments for support, ensuring reps prioritize productive interactions over unnecessary calls. Embracing virtual opportunities allows for the creation of a more effective sales task in the evolving work landscape.

Conducting virtual competency programs

If virtual components are integrated into your sales task, ensure that your reps are highly proficient in using virtual technologies. Merely relying on common tools like Zoom or Teams may fall short in the professional sales realm. Maintain high standards for virtual client interactions, equivalent to or exceeding those for in-person meetings. Consider aspects like appearance, emphasizing professional attire to convey credibility. Address technology needs, providing guidance on webcams, microphones, and internet quality for a polished virtual presence. Instruct reps on creating a professional virtual studio, including suitable lighting, background, and proper Zoom etiquette. Emphasize the importance of sales call planning for virtual interactions, covering document sharing, effective time management, and alignment with the sales task. Comprehensive training ensures reps excel in the dual opportunities and risks of virtual sales calling.

Creating virtual territories

Territories traditionally define a sales rep's scope based on geography, but in the virtual era, these boundaries can extend anywhere. To create virtual territories, assess the virtual sales task, considering increased call capacity due to reduced travel time. For instance, in a medical device scenario, reps making virtual calls could double their yearly outreach compared to in-person visits. While this offers flexibility, it's crucial to proceed gradually, allowing customers and reps to adapt. Consider a hybrid approach where occasional in-person visits maintain rapport. Avoid overly scattered virtual territories; keep reps calling in similar time zones or geographic regions to ensure familiarity with customers and regional nuances. Measure results, especially customer satisfaction, and periodically join virtual sales calls to monitor progress effectively. Engage relevant teams, like IT and supply chain, to align systems with the new virtual approach. Leadership and collaboration are pivotal for successful implementation.

Continuing your sales management journey

Sales managers are highly valued for their role in overseeing a company's sales force, making it one of the most crucial positions. To advance in sales management, continuously develop your professional skill set. Seek opportunities to broaden your experience, such as transitioning to marketing roles or taking on positions abroad or within special project teams. Embrace lifelong learning, stay updated on technology, explore best practices in other industries, and engage with professional organizations like the Sales Management Association. Actively participate in communities of practice, attend conferences, and network with peers. Learning involves taking action, reflecting, and improving. Experiment with new techniques, balance business needs with individual concerns, communicate honestly, build trust, and maintain a strong ethical foundation. Success in sales management is measured by ethical practices, not just accolades.

Chapter 2 Serving Customers in a Continuously Changing World

Addressing new safety protocols in your workplace

Putting "customers first" can be a powerful mantra, especially when safety is also a top priority. Balancing safety protocols with customer service requires understanding the importance of these precautions, embracing necessary adjustments, and avoiding common pitfalls. Internalizing the significance of safety measures, adapting processes, and maintaining a commitment to excellence will ensure a positive customer experience amid evolving challenges.

Overcoming new challenges with your customer service team members

A consulting client, a global cleaning products company, faced challenges due to backordered supplies amid increased demand. The sales team, unable to sell, pivoted to support production, exemplifying adaptability. In this evolving work environment, you may be adjusting to staff changes, remote work, and new procedures. Support new hires, maintain clear communication in remote work settings, and familiarize yourself with on-site changes. Embrace the new normal, socialize responsibly, and collaborate with the team to deliver excellent customer service while supporting one another.

Handling today's new onsite challenges in customer service

In-person customer service has changed significantly due to new safety measures and regulations, leading to heated interactions and, in some cases, violence. To navigate these situations safely, avoid discrimination, treat all customers with respect, and intervene if witnessing unfair treatment. Refrain from engaging in political conversations and politely deflect such inquiries. Prepare to handle customers who resist new policies, remaining calm and finding alternative solutions to ensure a positive customer experience. Anticipating challenges and discussing strategies with your team beforehand can help mitigate potential issues.

Communicating effectively with customers today

To enhance customer communication in the current environment, remember three key principles. First, practice active listening, even in written communication, by focusing on the customer's words and understanding their perspective. Second, show understanding by expressing empathy and assuring them they're not alone in facing challenges. Third, clarify their needs, expectations, and provide solutions, considering new procedures and restrictions. Effective communication can lead to better outcomes. Evaluate and apply these communication strategies to enhance your customer interactions.

Dealing with upset customers in today's environment

Navigating the current challenges in customer service, such as supply chain issues and upset customers, requires effective strategies. To reduce customer frustration by 80% or more, focus on managing expectations. Communicate openly about delays, offer alternative products, and follow up regularly. If a customer is already upset, follow these four steps: 1) Own any mistakes, avoiding blame; 2) Let the customer vent without interruption; 3) Reassure them of your commitment to excellent service; 4) Provide unexpected value, like a credit or extra service. Applying these techniques can enhance customer interactions amid today's uncertainties.

Incorporating flexibility into your customer service efforts

The rapidly changing landscape of customer service poses new challenges, from safety measures to dealing with more aggressive customers. To excel in this environment, incorporating flexibility into your customer service policies is crucial. Three effective ways to achieve this include implementing a flexible cancellation and refund policy, offering payment plans for higher ticket items, and avoiding hidden fees or additional charges related to pandemic effects. By prioritizing flexibility, you can enhance customer satisfaction, maintain loyalty, and ensure long-term profitability for your business.

The importance of a positive attitude in customer service today

Maintaining a positive attitude in the evolving customer service landscape is crucial for success. Consider strategies like dedicating an hour before your shift to activities that uplift you, such as exercise or meditation. Prioritize consuming positive content like podcasts or training videos before work. Ensure you eat a nutritious meal to avoid feeling irritable. Use breaks to reset, whether by walking outside, meditating, or engaging in positive activities. Focus on positive aspects during your workday, and seek lighthearted conversations with colleagues or managers. Experiment with these approaches to discover what works best for you.

Showing empathy in the new customer service reality

Consider the concept of the "window of perception." Picture yourself in a living room looking out a window, observing various details. Now, imagine being outside looking into the same window, seeing different aspects. This scenario reflects the diverse perspectives involved in addressing customer issues, especially with the current changes in our world. To effectively serve customers, embrace empathy by understanding their viewpoint before devising solutions. Implement empathy by putting yourself in the customer's shoes, sharing relatable experiences, and offering multiple solutions. This approach fosters understanding and enhances customer satisfaction amid evolving rules and protocols. Practice empathy for positive outcomes with customers and colleagues alike.

Anticipating what your customer needs in customer service today

To anticipate your customers' needs: prioritize safety concerns with measures like hand sanitizing stations, offer convenience despite challenges, such as out-of-stock items, and find ways to provide extraordinary value, especially during economic challenges. Adapt your approach to ensure a safe, convenient, and affordable experience for your customers in our evolving service landscape.

Chapter 3 Strategic Business Planning

The value of a strong strategic plan

Business development is a multifaceted concept with varied interpretations, often seen as sales, relationship-building, or actions to expand a business. In essence, it involves proactively seeking growth opportunities and aligning resources for success, collaborating across departments like sales, marketing, and product development. Strategic planning is crucial for effective business development, requiring a deep understanding of the company, industry, and external factors. Key strategic elements include knowing the company's vision and long-term goals, assessing the current state, analyzing the industry landscape, understanding internal processes and finances, and gaining an external perspective on societal, competitive, economic, and political trends. Successful business developers integrate these strategic pieces for informed decision-making and sustainable growth.

SWOT Analysis Template

Strengths:

- Advantages of proposition

- Capabilities

- Competitive advantages

- Unique selling points (USPs)

- Resources, assets, people

- Experience, knowledge, data

- Financial reserves, likely returns

- Marketing – reach, distribution, awareness

- Innovation aspects

- Location and geographical

- Price, value, quality

- Accreditations, qualifications, certifications

- Processes, systems, IT, communications

- Cultural, attitudinal, behavioral

- Management cover, succession

- Philosophy and values

Weaknesses:

- Gaps in capabilities

- Lack of competitive strength

- Reputation, presence, and reach

- Financials

- Own known vulnerabilities

- Timescales, deadlines, and pressures

- Cash flow, start-up cash-drain

- Continuity, supply chain robustness

- Effects on core activities, distraction

- Reliability of data, plan predictability

- Morale, commitment, leadership

- Accreditations, etc.

- Processes and systems, etc.

- Management cover, succession

Opportunities:

- Market developments

- Competitors' vulnerabilities

- Industry or lifestyle trends

- Technology development and innovation

- Global influences

- New markets, vertical, horizontal

- Niche target markets

- Geographical, export, import

- New USPs

- Tactics – surprise, major contracts

- Business and product development

- Information and research

- Partnerships, agencies, distribution

- Volumes, production, economies

- Seasonal, weather, fashion influences

- Political effects

- Legislative effects

- Environmental effects

- IT developments

- Competitor intentions – various

- Market demand

- New technologies, services, ideas

- Vital contracts and partners

- Sustaining internal capabilities

Threats:

- Obstacles faced

- Insurmountable weaknesses

- Loss of key staff

- Sustainable financial backing

- Economy – home, abroad

- Seasonality, weather effects

The systems thinking strategic plan

When it comes to strategic planning for business development, there are various models available. Traditional strategic plans suit organizations with specific goals and limited internal or external changes, while others are designed for those facing high volatility. For effective business development planning, a holistic approach is essential. A systems thinking strategic plan considers internal and external factors impacting your organization and business development. This active plan integrates different perspectives, remains adaptable to market changes, and becomes a daily part of your routine. Key sections include the desired state (ultimate vision), current state (starting point), key indicators (measurable outcomes), future external environmental scan (considering external changes), and the gap state (focused goals to bridge the current and desired states). Systems thinking strategic plans empower focused steps, ensuring a holistic process for surpassing business development goals.

Building your strategic planning team

To ensure successful implementation of your strategic plan, involve the people responsible early on. While it might be tempting to handle everything yourself, the complexity of business strategy requires a team effort. Consider your team members individually, focusing on their attitudes and willingness to contribute. Look for natural leaders who align with your vision. Assess each department's critical role and identify key individuals with insights into implementation. Assign specific roles and responsibilities to each team member, fostering a sense of importance and contribution. Strengthen team bonds through community-building activities, laughter, and team-building initiatives. Allow downtime and encourage relationships among team members. Follow your team's lead during the implementation phase, letting them drive meetings, updates, and milestones. By empowering your team and instilling a sense of ownership, you increase the chances of successful plan execution, taking your organization to new heights.

Understanding the desired state

The strategic plan acts as your roadmap, outlining where you aim to go and how to get there. Starting with the desired state, encompassing the vision, mission, core values, and long-term goals, this section serves as your ultimate destination and source of motivation. The vision articulates your aspirations for the future, providing a guiding force for decision-making. The mission outlines specific actions to realize the vision, specifying products, services, and target audience. Core values define your culture, embodying key principles. Long-term goals, being specific and measurable, prioritize efforts toward achieving the desired state. This comprehensive approach sets the foundation for building your strategic plan.

Developing your vision, mission, and purpose statement

Developing your organization's vision marks the initiation of the strategic planning process. The vision encapsulates your future aspirations, guiding decisions, communicating your essence to employees, and attracting customers. To create a compelling vision, set a timeframe, form a diverse team, brainstorm ideas about the company's future impact, aspirations, and desired identity. Take a break to refresh your perspective, then collaborate to narrow down recurring themes into a concise vision statement. Seek feedback from employees, customers, and vendors to refine the vision. Iterate through these steps until your vision aligns precisely with your aspirations.

Mission Statements articulate how an organization executes its vision. Examples include:

- LinkedIn: "Connect the world's professionals to make them more productive and successful."

- PayPal: "Build the web's most convenient, secure, cost-effective payment solution."

- 3M: "Improve Every Life through Innovative Giving in Education, Community, and the Environment."

- Home Depot: "Provide the highest level of service, the broadest selection of products, and the most competitive prices."

- American Red Cross: "Prevent and alleviate human suffering in the face of emergencies by mobilizing the power of volunteers and the generosity of donors."

- Toyota: "Attract and attain customers with high-valued products and services and the most satisfying ownership experience in America."

- L'Oréal: "Offering all women and men worldwide the best of cosmetics innovation in terms of quality, efficacy, and safety."

- Southwest Airlines: "Dedication to the highest quality of Customer Service delivered with a sense of warmth, friendliness, individual pride, and Company Spirit."

To craft your vision, envision the future of your company by considering its aspirations over the next few years. Here are examples:

- Microsoft: "A computer on every desk and in every home."

- Nike: "Bring inspiration and innovation to every athlete in the world."

- McDonald's: "To be the world's best quick-service restaurant experience."

Your vision should be concise, inspiring, stable, challenging, and reflective of your company's purpose. Ask yourself questions like:

1. What do we want to achieve?

2. How do we help our clients?

3. What problems do we solve?

4. What are our strengths?

5. How do we improve lives?

6. What is our dream for the company?

7. How do we make a difference?

8. In five years, what impact do we want to have?

9. Where do we make the biggest impact?

10. What does our company stand for?

After answering these questions:

1. Identify repeated themes or phrases.

2. Answer the question "In five years, we will have?" multiple times.

3. Review and add details related to customers, employees, and community.

4. Repeat the process until you formulate a phrase that inspires and motivates you.

Designing your core values

The mission statement articulates the purpose of your business, outlining what it offers, whom it serves, the problems it solves, and how it accomplishes its vision. To create a robust mission statement:

1. Review mission statements from admired companies.

2. Answer key questions about your company's offerings, target customers, benefits to customers, and problems addressed.

3. Draft your mission statement, understanding that refinement will be necessary.

Following the mission statement, develop core values, the guiding principles of your business. This process involves:

1. Identifying the team members involved in the discussion.

2. Scheduling a brainstorming session to discuss your company's identity, priorities, commitments, and expectations.

3. Creating a long list of resonant words and phrases.

4. Narrowing down the list to a concise set of no more than five core values.

Examples of Core Values:

Use these examples as a starting point to brainstorm your core values—the principles you uphold, the commitments you make to customers, and the criteria for evaluating performance.

- Innovation

- Creativity

- Energy

- Integrity

- Positive Attitude

- Service Excellence

- Optimism

- Compassion

- Humor

- Adventurous Spirit

- Proactive Thinking

- Resilience

- Accuracy

- Attention to Detail

- Perseverance

- Dependability

- Loyalty

- Courage

- Health

- Fun

- Dedication

- Passion

- Education

- Focus

- Growth

How to Determine Your Core Values:

Core values can be a single word, a few words, or a phrase—expressing what is crucial to your business and your commitments to customers, employees, and yourself.

1. Review your vision and mission.

2. Identify values aligned with your vision and mission.

3. Consider any additional values important to your business.

4. Answer key questions:

  - What do you prioritize beyond financial success?

  - What behaviors do you reward?

  - What qualities do you admire in your team members?

  - What five words would you want customers to use in describing you?

  - What promises would you make to customers and employees?

5. Identify the top five values that consistently appear in your responses.

6. Refine and repeat the process until you have your top five values.

The future external environmental scan

When crafting strategic plans, it's natural to focus inward on our business goals. However, to ensure the plan's success, understanding external factors is crucial. The Future External Environmental Scan (FEES) guides this exploration, encompassing society, customers, politics, economy, technology, and industry. By dedicating time to each area with a diverse team, you gain insights into external changes and trends. This awareness allows proactive adjustments to your strategic plan, transforming potential threats into opportunities.

Future Trends Analysis

Identify and analyze five to ten future external environmental trends using the SKEPTIC framework:

- Society: Consider demographic shifts and a faster-paced, results-driven society.

- Competition: Evaluate collaborative efforts and potential decreases in competitors.

- Economics: Examine economic challenges and a shift towards local importance.

- Political/Regulatory: Assess factors like tax credits and governmental budget cuts.

- Technology: Explore advancements such as cell phone applications and virtual client meetings.

- Industry: Look into emerging products, services, and increased contract labor.

- Customers: Analyze changes in customer behavior, emphasizing education and a slower response.

Setting strategic long-term goals

In the desired state, the final step involves setting long-term goals, marking the initiation of actionable steps in the strategic planning process. These goals play a crucial role in realizing the vision and mission while upholding core values. Distinguishing between short-term and long-term goals is essential. While short-term goals are specific, measurable, and attainable within a shorter timeframe, long-term goals span three to five years. For instance, a long-term goal might be to increase sales by 25% in three years, while a corresponding short-term goal could involve defining the sales process and hiring a leader within three months.

To establish effective long-term goals, alignment with the vision, mission, and core values is paramount. Start by reviewing these foundational elements and ask, "If this is what we aim to achieve, what steps are required?" An example from a financial services firm illustrates this synergy:

- Vision: To help customers achieve a lifetime of success.

- Mission: Provide financial services that enhance lives, increase and protect wealth.

- Core Values: Uncompromising integrity, lifelong relationships, work harder and smarter, proactive service, committed partnership.

Long-term goals for this firm include expanding private client services, increasing client relationship depth, developing new product lines, enhancing customer experience, creating a top-client-specific website, and upgrading training and development.

For long-term goals to be effective, they must be not only aligned but also specific and measurable. The more specificity and clarity in your goals, the better you can measure and, consequently, achieve success.

Short-Term Goals:

Embarking on the exciting phase of strategic planning, it's time to craft your short-term goals. Begin by revisiting your SEEDs, WEEDs, NEEDs, and SWOT analyses, along with your future state encompassing vision, mission, values, and long-term goals. Follow these steps:

1. Identify your significant areas of need by examining SEEDs, WEEDs, NEEDs, and SWOT.

2. Consider the first three essential actions that come to mind when envisioning your desired state.

3. Combine both lists into one comprehensive list.

4. Prioritize the list and take a break; revisit it later to ensure alignment.

5. Review the list again to confirm the priorities.

6. Select the top three priorities as your short-term goals.

Long-Term Goals:

When contemplating your long-term goals, it's crucial to align them with your vision, mission, and values. Follow these steps:

1. Review your vision, mission, and values.

2. Brainstorm the necessary steps to achieve these goals within your company.

3. Prioritize the identified steps.

4. Transform them into measurable objectives.

5. Select the top five priorities as your long-term goals.

Determine your current state

To chart a course for the future, start by evaluating where you presently stand. Conduct a thorough and candid examination of your business, addressing what's effective, what's not, and potential concerns. Identifying advantages is crucial for strategic planning. Two tools for an in-depth analysis are the traditional SWOT Analysis, encompassing strengths, weaknesses, opportunities, and threats, and the current state analysis, which delves into both internal and external factors. The SWOT Analysis aims to leverage strengths, mitigate weaknesses, capitalize on opportunities, and recognize threats for effective management and growth.

1. Strengths: Identify the robust aspects of your business, such as longevity, high customer satisfaction, or consistent profitability over the years.

2. Weaknesses: Address challenges like low employee morale, the need for enhanced customer relationships, outdated technology, or a lack of bench strength.

3. Opportunities: Envision promising avenues, such as opening new markets, refining sales techniques, or developing innovative products.

4. Threats: Recognize external factors that could impact your business negatively, like new competitors, economic shifts, or rising resource costs.

Completing this analysis provides a foundation for understanding your current state, paving the way for effective growth management.

Creating your key strategic initiatives

Start with the end goal in mind – a phrase I truly appreciate. Once you've established the desired state with the vision, mission, values, and long-term goals, the next step is crucial. It's time to delve into the key strategic initiatives, a detailed exploration of how things will look once you've achieved your goals. These initiatives go beyond the surface, detailing the changes, impacts, and unique features your company will embody. While it might seem superficial initially, it's essential to take it seriously, as these initiatives form the vivid narrative of your business's future. Picture the transformation: increased business, expanded markets, enhanced benefits, or more leisure time. To initiate your key strategic initiatives, start by pondering these questions: What notable changes will occur in your company? What achievements will you unlock? What impact will your strategy have on your business, community, and personal life? What practices or outcomes will be discontinued?

Envision your Key Strategic Initiatives:

1. Team Transformation: Envision the positive changes in your team.

2. Customer Base: Picture the types of customers you'll draw in.

3. Company Evolution: Imagine the transformative journey of your company.

4. Personal Impact: Envision the changes in your personal life.

5. Team Composition: Define the individuals comprising your team.

6. Attracted Talent: Consider the kind of talent you'll attract.

7. Activities Reduction: Identify aspects you'll do less of.

8. Increased Activities: Envision what you'll do more of.

9. Overcome Challenges: Visualize challenges that will be resolved.

10. Competitor Landscape: Define your competitors or their absence.

Using your SWOT to close the gap

The SWOT analysis provides a broad overview of your current state, but for a deeper understanding of your company's challenges and opportunities, utilize the SEEDs, WEEDs, and NEEDs tool.

SEEDs, WEEDs, and NEEDs are strategic planning concepts used to identify and categorize internal and external factors that can influence an organization's strategic direction.

1. SEEDs (Strengths, Experience, Expertise, and Differentiators):

  - Strengths:

    - Established brand reputation

    - High-quality products/services

    - Strong financial position

    - Skilled and motivated workforce

  - Experience:

    - Decades of industry experience

    - Proven track record in customer satisfaction

    - Successful execution of past projects

  - Expertise:

    - Specialized knowledge in a niche market

- Cutting-edge technology expertise

- Industry thought leadership

- Differentiators:

- Unique selling propositions

- Innovative product features

- Exclusive partnerships

2. WEEDs (Weaknesses, Errors, Efficiencies, and Deficiencies):

- Weaknesses:

- Limited brand awareness

- Dependence on a single supplier

- Lack of diversification in product offerings

- Errors:

- Historical mistakes in marketing strategy

- Product recalls or quality issues

- Mismanagement of customer relationships

- Efficiencies:

- Inefficient business processes

- Outdated technology infrastructure

- High production costs

- Deficiencies:

- Insufficient employee training programs

- Poor internal communication

- Inadequate succession planning

3. NEEDs (Needs, Expectations, External Factors, and Demand):

- Needs:

  - Changing customer needs and preferences

  - Emerging trends that create new demands

  - Evolving regulatory requirements

- Expectations:

  - Increasing customer expectations for sustainability

  - Market expectations for innovation

  - Growing demand for corporate social responsibility

- External Factors:

  - Economic shifts affecting consumer purchasing power

  - Political changes impacting industry regulations

  - Technological advancements disrupting traditional markets

- Demand:

  - Fluctuations in market demand for specific products

  - Seasonal variations in consumer demand

  - Shifts in demographic patterns influencing demand

This tool helps identify strengths (SEEDs) to nurture, weaknesses (WEEDs) to address, and needs (NEEDs) crucial for achieving your desired growth.

1. SEEDs (Step 2):

   - Identify what is working well in your company.

   - Determine areas that demand continued focus and investment.

   - Example: A redesigned sales team generating impressive results.

2. WEEDs (Step 3):

   - Recognize elements impeding progress and tying you down.

   - Address weaknesses that hinder overall advancement.

- Example: Acknowledge and resolve leadership obstacles hindering marketing team progress.

3. NEEDs (Step 4):

   - Pinpoint essentials crucial for realizing your desired state.

   - Allocate resources, time, and energy to meet these needs.

   - Example: Invest in opening new markets or upgrading technology.

This comprehensive approach prepares you to take strategic steps toward achieving your desired state.

SEEDs, WEEDs, NEEDs Tool Overview:

SEEDs:

- Identify what contributes to growth and success.

- Examples: Strong team, loyal customers, consistent growth.

WEEDs:

- Recognize obstacles and factors impeding progress.

- Examples: Office drama, lack of technology.

NEEDs:

- Identify essential elements lacking for enhanced productivity.

- Examples: Bench strength, access to new markets.

Consider each aspect in detail and utilize the insights to:

- Prioritize tasks.

- Allocate resources effectively.

- Address immediate concerns.

- Identify lacking resources needed to tackle problems and priorities.

Executing your strategic plan

The ultimate objective of any strategic plan is successful implementation, and the key component that transitions you from planning to execution is the focus on short-term goals. These goals are the initial steps that bridge the gap between your current state and the desired state outlined in your strategic plan. For instance, if a long-term goal involves expanding into new markets, but current markets are not yet profitable, short-term goals may include achieving profitability in all markets within six months and conducting research to determine the most viable expansion targets. Short-term goals essentially serve as mini-strategic plans, directing your efforts toward narrowing the gap between your current and desired states. To get started, assess your desired state for the next three to five years and your current state. Brainstorm and list the actions required to move closer to your desired state. Prioritize these actions, identify the most impactful ones, and select the top three as your short-term goals.

Developing metrics and accountability

You've crafted an impressive strategic plan, but the challenge lies in transitioning from planning to execution. The key to making your strategic plan effective is to develop action plans – detailed, step-by-step strategies designed for short-term goals. Action plans are essential for implementation, focusing on small, manageable chunks of the overall plan. Ensure your short-term goals are measurable, establish specific timeframes, and determine when to start and finish. Break down each goal into detailed steps, making them measurable and assigning responsibilities. Create measurements and accountability to track progress and achieve desired results.

Action Plan Example

- Short-term goal: Increase sales by [Percentage]%.

- Start time: [Month, Year]

Action Steps

1. Define your target market.

2. Update all prospects lists to reach [Number of Prospects].

3. Identify [Number of Referral] sources.

Measurement

1. I have a prospect list completed those fits my target market.

2. I have identified and contacted my referral sources.

Accountability

1. Sales increase.

2. Everyone on our team understands and knows the target market.

It's your turn. Your action plans will be more detailed, but use this as a starting point.

Creating ownership of your strategic plan

To effectively implement your strategic plan, it's crucial to create ownership among your team. Team members who are actively involved in the planning process are more likely to be engaged in its success. Identify key team members, encourage their involvement, and ask questions to give them a voice and responsibility. Utilize strategic planning tools like future external environmental scans, SEEDs, WEEDs, and NEEDs, and SWOT analysis to gather feedback and enhance communication. Regularly discuss, focus on, and update the plan based on team input to ensure ongoing success.

Keeping the strategic plan active

Implementing a strategic plan can be challenging, often leading plans to be forgotten and unused. To overcome this, delegate responsibility for short-term goals, appoint owners, and form task forces to execute the work. Establish a structured system for updates and progress checks, preferably quarterly, with consistency in reporting formats. This approach ensures continuous focus on the plan, facilitating steady progress and implementation.

Activate Your Strategic Plan:

Steps:

1. Empower Ownership: Assign dedicated team members to take ownership of the strategic plan. Leverage the principle that people support what they help create.

2. Form Task Force: Assemble a task force comprising individuals from key departments crucial for plan success. Ensure representation at various organizational levels.

3. Develop Structure: Design the framework for your plan's execution, including meeting schedules, milestones, and reporting mechanisms.

Questions for Designing Your Structure:

- What are the long-term and short-term goals?

- How frequently should meetings occur?

- Where will meetings take place (boardrooms, off-site, virtual)?

- Who should be present at the meetings?

- What information will be reported (milestones, updates, wins/losses)?

- How will success be measured after each meeting?

- What are the consequences for non-participation, lack of reporting, or insufficient progress?

- Who will assume accountability?

Five pitfalls of business development strategic planning

Strategic planning can be a source of frustration for many organizations, facing roadblocks that hinder successful implementation. Here are five common challenges and strategies to overcome them:

1. Complexity Overload:

   - Challenge: Plans become too intricate, hindering understanding and execution.

   - Strategy: Simplify your strategic plan, focusing on three to five short-term goals with manageable action steps for each.

2. Lack of Implementation Planning:

   - Challenge: Failing to create a structured implementation plan after developing the strategic plan.

   - Strategy: Develop a clear roadmap for executing your strategic plan, defining roles, responsibilities, and reporting structures.

3. Inadequate Team Alignment:

- Challenge: Selecting the wrong individuals for plan execution, lacking ownership.

- Strategy: Ensure strategic plan ownership at the top of the organization and carefully assign team members who can contribute effectively.

4. Rigidity in Planning:

- Challenge: A plan that doesn't adapt to changes in the business environment.

- Strategy: Build flexibility into your strategic plan, allowing adjustments to capitalize on opportunities and navigate threats.

5. Lack of Honesty:

- Challenge: Failing to be brutally honest about challenges, weaknesses, and goals.

- Strategy: Embrace honesty during the planning process, acknowledging challenges and weaknesses, as this transparency is crucial for effective action.

These strategies aim to guide organizations past common roadblocks, fostering a greater chance of successful strategic plan implementation.

Chapter 4 Maintaining Account Relationships

Why is this important?

Why focus on maintaining relationships with client's post-sale? While the initial sale is complete, ongoing value addition is crucial. Continuing to respond promptly, matching solutions to problems, and showcasing product value helps maintain the relationship. This approach offers key advantages: the opportunity for upselling, protecting customers from competitors, avoiding buyer's remorse, and gaining referrals. Building and nurturing these relationships contribute to sustained business growth and client satisfaction.

Make it personal

After completing the sales process, your personal relationship with the client should deepen. Despite the initial aversion to trusting salespeople, the sale signifies a shift. With the financial incentive gone, it's an opportune time to transition from a business associate to a genuine friend and trusted collaborator. In-person meetings or social media provide avenues to learn about personal interests, hobbies, family, and other relevant details. Authentic connections, based on shared interests, contribute to stronger relationships and facilitate future conversations and engagements.

Keep it professional

While building a personal connection is vital for a lasting relationship, maintaining professionalism is crucial in a business setting. Prioritizing a strong professional relationship before a personal one ensures a solid foundation. Seeking feedback on the overall experience with the company, personal interactions, and the product or service helps improve and eliminate potential issues. Understanding the broader team within the client's company expands touchpoints and strengthens connections. Analogously, envisioning each team member as a 'tooth' in a cog emphasizes the importance of multiple connections for smoother collaboration and a robust relationship.

Become an active listener

In nurturing both personal and professional relationships with existing customers, active listening is essential. Many salespeople tend to focus on constant pitching and showcasing value, but the key lies in understanding the customer's problems and providing tailored solutions. Post-sale, it becomes even more critical to listen and adapt to evolving challenges. Requesting feedback and genuinely considering both positive and negative aspects helps gain insights into their needs. Additionally, asking 'why' to understand the significance of feedback, complaints, and their choice of your service enhances your ability to sustain the relationship and consistently add value.

Two-way referring

A valuable practice is engaging in two-way referrals—referring your customers to your network and vice versa. This mutually beneficial approach enhances customer satisfaction, expands your network, and fosters goodwill. Referrals are seen as compliments, and the positive impact ripples through all parties involved. Consider referring clients to potential contacts in various professional and personal spheres, reinforcing your relationships and creating opportunities for reciprocal gestures that can further benefit your business.

Treat them

When treating prospects, the approach can either strengthen the relationship for future sales and referrals or be perceived as a desperate sales attempt, pushing them away. To do it right, consider their preferences, whether it's a physical treat or experience. Match the treat to their interests or what they've shared. Document this information for future reference, such as for holiday gifts or event invitations. Tailoring your gestures shows thoughtfulness and enhances the relationship, fostering positive outcomes.

Meet them

When arranging a meal or meeting at a venue, consider the client's preferences, dietary restrictions, geography, and cost. Arrive early to choose an ideal location within the venue. Exercise caution with alcohol consumption to maintain professionalism. Keep your phone away to demonstrate undivided attention during the meeting. This ensures a positive and respectful interaction with the client.

Keep it regular

To maintain momentum in building customer relationships, schedule regular recurring meetings rather than one-time interactions. Consider meeting quarterly as a good balance to stay on their radar without being too frequent. Avoid using every meeting for sales pitches; instead, use some to build friendships and inquire about their well-being.

Avoid bribery

Caution is essential when cultivating personal relationships with clients to avoid crossing into bribery territory. Local laws and company policies should be thoroughly understood to establish appropriate boundaries. Avoid making explicit agreements that link personal gestures to business outcomes, as this could be interpreted as bribery. Acts of kindness and relationship-building should be genuine, without expectations of a specific business return.

Set reminders

Utilize technology to build relationships effectively, starting with a simple calendar. Record important dates such as birthdays, promotions, and personal milestones, and set reminders for easy recall. Take it a step further by researching their interests, like sports events or hobbies. When reminders prompt you, reach out with genuine, non-sales communication to strengthen the relationship. Show that you remembered and care, fostering a positive connection beyond sales pitches.

Going rotten timers

To avoid deals going stale, consider using specialized software with built-in timers that reset with each contact or update. This prevents prospects from forgetting about you and turning to competitors. Sales CRM software offer this functionality. You can customize the duration of the timer based on your industry's dynamics, ensuring timely follow-ups and keeping relationships fresh.

Recommended CRMs with 'Going Rotten' Feature:

1. Pipedrive: Highlights deals going rotten, allowing customization of the rotten point duration. Visualizes deals in red past the specified time.

2. HubSpot: While lacking a 'going rotten' feature, it tracks the 'Last Activity Date,' helping assess deal freshness based on recent interactions.

3. Freshsales: Lets you set a custom 'Deals Rot After' timer in days, highlighting rotten deals in red within the Open Deals section. These CRMs offer effective tools for managing deal lifecycles."

Document everything

When leveraging software and tools for efficiency, a crucial reminder is to consistently document information. While some salespeople excel at retaining details mentally, for most, relying on notes is essential. A robust CRM with a reliable search function negates the need to memorize extensive details about customers, enabling quick access to information. However, the 'garbage in, garbage out' principle applies—keeping data disorganized or neglecting documentation hinders retrieval when needed. Maintain uniform and comprehensive notes, covering basics like name, role, phone number, and expand based on personal preferences or shared interests, ensuring a well-organized and informative CRM.

Not delivering on promised value

Whether the fault lies with suppliers, colleagues, or oneself, it's crucial to navigate delivery issues effectively. As reputable salespeople, preserving our name, securing return business, and fostering a positive reputation are paramount. The upcoming sections focus on taking ownership of mistakes, rectifying the situation, and implementing measures to prevent recurrence.

Owning your mistakes

When facing a delivery issue, it's crucial to immediately take ownership, regardless of the source of the mistake. Whether it originated from a colleague, supplier, junior staff, or even your boss, as the person maintaining the customer relationship, it's your responsibility. Apologize sincerely, refrain from assigning blame, and assure the customer that you are committed to investigating and resolving the problem. Avoid pointing fingers, as it can create an impression of a lack of control and undermine your team. Position yourself as an internal advocate, promising to delve into the issue, engage the necessary parties, and oversee a swift resolution. Handling mistakes with honesty and integrity not only demonstrates your humanity but also strengthens client relationships, paving the way for return business, referrals, and positive sentiments.

Making it right

Once we've acknowledged and owned the mistake, the next step is making it right. Contrary to impulsively offering discounts or panicking, the focus should be on efficiently resolving the issue and rebuilding trust. While incentives may be warranted in significant cases, avoid making it a knee-jerk reaction, as it can lead to undervaluing your products or services. After resolving the problem, consider expressing gratitude for the customer's patience with a thoughtful reward—a one-time discount, a gift, a freebie, or a lunch. This should be a personal gesture, reflecting sincere appreciation rather than desperation to retain the customer. However, the key to lasting success is preventing a recurrence of the issue.

Don't let it happen again

After successfully resolving the issue, the focus shifts to preventing a recurrence. While mistakes are inevitable, handling them well involves learning and improvement. Identify why the problem occurred, pinpoint the stage in the process, and determine responsibility. Assess whether training or a new system can address the issue. Stay closely involved to ensure it doesn't happen again. Communicate your commitment to personal responsibility and transparency with the customer. Avoid repeating the same mistake to maintain trust and credibility.

Post-Sale Summary

We covered key strategies for post-sale relationship maintenance. Emphasizing relationship selling, personalized and thoughtful interactions, efficient automation, and effective resolution of delivery issues. Focus on what your prospect values, engage in reciprocal referrals, leverage notes and calendars for personalized engagement, use software to monitor deals, take ownership of mistakes, and avoid repeating them. Lastly, refrain from immediate discounts; instead, reward customers after resolving issues.

Chapter 5 Business to Consumer Online Sales

Going straight to the consumer

Many companies are now choosing to sell directly to consumers online due to the following reasons: firstly, it aligns with the significant presence of customers on the internet; secondly, it provides accessibility without a substantial financial investment; and thirdly, it allows businesses to cater to a global audience. While direct-to-consumer sales were once viewed skeptically, the landscape has shifted, with online platforms offering profitability, productivity, and enhanced customer service. The prevalence of online shopping is evident, with 79% of US consumers shopping online or via mobile devices, a significant increase from 22% in 2000. According to Statistica, an estimated 2.1 billion people globally will engage in online shopping by 2021. Cost is identified as the primary reason for consumers choosing to shop online, surpassing convenience. Despite the logical reasoning associated with cost, understanding that buying decisions are rooted in the limbic system is crucial. Strategies to address cost concerns will be explored in later lessons. As consumers increasingly seek online options, businesses must adapt to this changing buying behavior by establishing a compelling online presence.

Categories of online B2C companies

While it's commonly advised for offline businesses to establish an online presence, not all online businesses can seamlessly transition offline. Certain jobs, such as mechanics, dog groomers, or caregivers, necessitate physical presence. Despite the increasing popularity of online shopping, many consumers still express a preference for brick-and-mortar businesses. Offline businesses face challenges like infrastructure costs and limited access to online shoppers. However, having a strong online presence remains crucial for brand credibility. A robust online brand can complement offline campaigns and promotions, driving traffic, brand awareness, and conversions. Conversely, well-crafted offline campaigns can boost web traffic and fuel automated online campaigns, creating a powerful synergy. Integrating online and offline efforts can enhance brand representation, deliver valuable content, and contribute to increased profitability with the target audience.

Categories of offline B2C companies

B2C e-commerce refers to the electronic relationship between businesses and end consumers. Today, nearly every product or service available offline can also be found online, from consumer goods on Amazon to groceries, cars, homes, travel planning, legal and financial services, healthcare scheduling, and entertainment streaming. Offering products and services online provides immediate access to information for consumers, enhancing value, customer service, and quality. Your company can likely benefit significantly by establishing an online presence.

Opportunities and challenges

On the positive side, online platforms attract 80% of consumers seeking products or services. While the challenge is to resist the allure of physical distribution, direct online marketing proves cost-effective and profitable. Online B-to-C offers constant accessibility, 24/7, enhancing profitability and scalability. The low entry cost and global reach further make it a compelling option. On the downside, expect higher return rates, but with effective customer targeting, increased profitability offsets the costs. The main drawback is inevitable price comparisons, yet addressing consumer psychology can mitigate this. Overall, the advantages of online B-to-C, including global access and cost-effectiveness, make it a valuable avenue for business growth.

What is a persona?

Ever had a conversation where someone wrongly assumes they understand your thoughts and feelings? It's irritating, especially when they're trying to sell you something. Enter personas: in sales and marketing, they represent a generalized image of your ideal customer. Building accurate personas involves direct communication with existing customers through interviews, web forms, surveys, and analytics. This insight enables targeted, personalized content delivery to different customer segments. Buyer personas ensure your message aligns with the right audience at the right time. Negative personas help filter out less likely customers, optimizing time and resources. Crafting detailed buyer personas, combined with understanding decision-making neuroscience, allows you to effectively speak to potential buyers and deliver tailored content throughout the buying cycle, optimizing efforts for good leads and customer retention.

How do I build personas?

Developing buyer personas is more art than science, but it's crucial to apply rigor in defining characteristics of your various buyers. The ideal number of personas varies, typically ranging from four to six, following the 80-20 rule. Negative personas should also be considered. Start by examining existing customers, utilizing online templates for guidance. Ask detailed questions about both work and personal lives to create a comprehensive portrait. Seek input from your sales team and others in direct customer contact. Web forms on your site can collect demographic information, while website analytics offer insights into visitor behavior. Naming and describing personas, such as "IT John" or "VP Marketing Mark," aids visualization. Tailor personas for each online and social media channel to target customer interests effectively. Crafting accurate personas enables targeted communication comparable to face-to-face interactions.

What are the secrets to persona success?

Creating buyer personas is not just about identifying your ideal customer; success lies in effectively reaching them with the right message at different stages of their buyer journey. Key success factors include keeping personas realistic, avoiding idealized versions, and incorporating negative personas to identify customers you don't want. Negative personas help filter out unqualified leads, saving resources. Start small with two or three buyer personas and one or two negative personas, avoiding the confusion of creating too many. Remember, personas are general representations, not specific individuals. Regularly revisit and refine personas to enhance accuracy and success. Utilize free online resources to guide and improve your persona creation process.

Measure persona success

Success with personas hinges on consistently identifying, attracting, engaging, and winning your target personas at every sales cycle stage. Correctly targeting personas should lead to increased traffic and conversion at a lower cost. If results are lacking, trust your persona development but refine your reach and content delivery. Analytics and SEO reveal how content is consumed, aiding in delivering relevant content throughout the sales cycle. A/B testing helps optimize content effectiveness, resulting in more qualified leads and conversions. Heat maps, combined with SEO, provide insights into consumer engagement. If results are unsatisfactory, revisiting and refining personas may be necessary. Avoid the mistake of creating personas based on assumptions; research and utilize available online resources for accurate and valuable personas. The effort invested in persona development will yield significant rewards.

Why content equals sales success

In online consumer outreach, content is paramount because it shapes your identity and engages the buyer's brain. Studies indicate that 70% prefer information from articles over advertisements. The key to great content lies in capturing attention quickly, given humans' dwindling attention spans. Every element, from headlines to visuals, must collaborate to guide the buyer effectively. The F pattern is a favorable layout, aligning with online consumer behavior. Well-designed infographics and websites effectively capture attention and engage the buying brain. Creating compelling content, especially on your website, is crucial for sustained business success.

Where do I start with my website copy?

To sell effectively on your website, tell compelling stories rather than focusing solely on product features. Examples like Dove's sketches, VW's Star Wars, and Apple's 1984 ad showcase the power of emotional storytelling. Neuroscience reveals that the buying brain resides in the limbic system, where emotions are processed. Understanding buyer personas and utilizing social triggers such as reciprocation, commitment, and consistency enhances your storytelling impact. Design your content following established patterns like the F pattern or Z pattern, guiding the buyer's brain seamlessly. Remember, the purpose of every word and image is to lead the reader forward. Crafting stories that resonate with your target audience and address problems before presenting solutions significantly boosts website conversion success.

What are the secrets to content success?

Bad design and poorly written copy aren't just ineffective; they harm your business by reflecting poorly on your brand. It's crucial to create content that speaks to your target personas' buying brain. While simplicity is essential, achieving brevity requires clarity and discipline. Strive for brevity and clarity, understanding that it takes time. Short copy lacking substance is meaningless, while long, irrelevant copy goes unread. Relevance surpasses brevity, and copy should be precisely as long as needed. Copy becomes too long when people stop reading it. Tools can help gauge consumer engagement, and Joe Sugarman's advice emphasizes the importance of the first sentence leading to the next for effective communication with the buying brain. Success lies in keeping communication clear, simple, and concise while creating copy and design that connects directly with the target audience. Consistent execution of the call to action indicates the right track, while adjustments may be needed for desired results.

Measure content success

Success is measurable through analytics like A/B testing and optimization. Understanding and honing personas based on their responses is crucial. Search Engine Optimization (SEO) involves tailoring website copy for better search engine visibility, considering what personas search for and using analytics tools like Google Analytics and AdWords. Utilizing tools such as Optimizely and Crazy Egg, along with easy-to-use tools like Google URL Builder and Google URL Shortener, allows tracking conversions and engagement. Regularly revisiting and refining personas, testing, and optimizing copy and design are essential. Analyzing target personas ensures effective communication. The discussed analytical and testing tools provide real-time data to adjust strategies for optimal engagement. The formula for success is simple: analyze, test, optimize, and repeat.

What is social media marketing?

Social media encompasses various electronic communication forms, not just popular platforms like Facebook or Twitter. Social media marketing involves using platforms to garner website traffic or brand attention. Billions of people are active on social media, and it has become a primary way consumers search for products and educate themselves. Creating a social media presence is essential, as it provides access to a vast audience with analytics for targeted outreach. Blogging significantly boosts lead generation and strengthens your brand's credibility. Utilizing review sites like Yelp and Google+ Local aids online reputation management and reduces negative reviews. Given that 80% of consumers spend time on social media, showing up there is crucial for success.

Social media marketing

Establishing an effective social media and website traffic strategy for your business may seem daunting, but it can be manageable with a step-by-step approach. Begin by creating business profiles on platforms like Facebook, LinkedIn, Twitter, and YouTube, ensuring links between your website and social media pages. Incorporate an easily accessible blog into your website's navigation. Develop a content calendar to streamline content sharing on various social media sites, optimizing the message's timing and placement. Leverage existing content, such as presentations and articles, and repurpose them for blogs and social sites. Infographics are highly shareable and contribute valuable content. Utilize your personas and available resources to kickstart your strategy efficiently.

Secrets to social media success

Achieving success in social media relies on planning, engagement, and responsiveness. A content calendar is crucial, as companies with documented marketing plans are 60% more likely to succeed in content marketing. The calendar helps focus on content creation, optimize resources, and prevent gaps in content delivery, improving visibility and SEO rankings. Staying engaged involves monitoring and analyzing responses through various analytics tools provided by social media platforms. Effective social media creates a two-way conversation, and being responsive to consumer comments fosters great customer service, offering valuable insights for relevant content creation. Planning, engagement, and responsiveness significantly enhance the chances of success in social media marketing.

Measure social media success

To accurately gauge the success of your social media marketing, start by clarifying your goals. Key metrics include reach (number of people who saw your content) and impressions (how many times it was displayed). Engagement metrics, such as shares, likes, and comments, provide insights into brand awareness and content interest. However, prioritize metrics aligned with your business goals, like follower growth, increased website traffic, and conversions.

Google Analytics is a valuable tool for measuring social media's impact on conversions. While conversions are crucial, also consider measuring reach, influence, and engagement. Don't abandon content or platforms solely based on conversion metrics; other factors, like increased brand awareness, matter. Always measure what aligns with your objectives and recognize that building a meaningful following takes time.

What is PPC?

Now that you've defined your personas, crafted your content, and shared it, if your website traffic is sluggish, consider Pay-Per-Click (PPC). Unlike Search Engine Optimization (SEO), PPC allows you to buy specific keywords and phrases, delivering quick and targeted results. While SEO is crucial for long-term success, PPC offers immediate visibility, potentially increasing traffic and conversions overnight. It provides precise targeting options, reaching your personas where and when they are most active. Affordable and scalable, PPC ensures you only pay when someone clicks on your ad, offering control over your budget and allowing measurement of campaign performance. With a quick start, clear cost visibility, and measurable results, PPC can be an effective solution, especially when speed is essential.

Where to start with PPC?

PPC success starts with identifying ideal keywords. Analyze popular keywords from your analytics and consider using autocomplete suggestions from search engines. Time-consuming but crucial, finding the right keywords is vital for PPC success. Determine your budget, bid on chosen keywords, and set the amount you're willing to pay per click. Control the message with a compelling headline, but be honest to avoid negative outcomes. Monitor results closely and optimize regularly, as PPC can generate fast traffic but requires ongoing attention. If clicks don't convert, adjust ads, try different keywords, or pause campaigns that aren't delivering results. In PPC, success depends on staying vigilant and adapting strategies based on real-time insights.

What are the secrets to PPC success?

To increase PPC success, first, understand its purpose—ideal for quick visibility boosts, such as new campaigns or product launches. Vigilance is key; monitor results regularly to ensure cost-effectiveness. Use analytics from platforms like Google AdWords for insights. Focus on conversions, not just click-through rates.

Test ads and keywords, and explore multiple search engines. Landing pages enhance campaigns and aid SEO efforts. In summary, PPC is easy but requires planning, close monitoring, and data-driven optimization for web traffic success.

Measure the success of PPC

Measure PPC success with click-through rate (CTR), which reveals ad relevance. Prioritize conversion, ensuring the desired action is taken. Monitor cost per conversion to evaluate customer acquisition cost. Utilize negative keywords to filter out unlikely converters. Quality score, assessing keyword, ad, and landing page relevance, impacts ad placement and cost per click. Regularly optimize content and strategy for better results. Used effectively, PPC can rapidly boost traffic and conversions. Consider professional help if needed, but proactive research and optimization can lead to successful PPC outcomes.

Next steps

Start by creating buyer personas to understand your target customers. Develop a content calendar for strategic content delivery throughout the sales cycle. Testing and optimization are key to refining your approach based on data. Effective content, combined with SEO and PPC knowledge, sets the foundation for success in online B2C. Analyze, test, optimize, and repeat for ongoing success in building your online presence.

Chapter 6 Managing Your Sales Process

Why a sales process is key

Life is filled with routines, or processes, that we often take for granted. These are essentially habits we've developed, like the routine we follow when coming home from work. In sales, where numerous tasks demand attention, having a structured sales process is crucial. It enhances efficiency, organizes company roles, boosts revenue, and improves forecasting accuracy. Some may find the idea uncomfortable, but a well-established sales process is key to a salesperson's success, providing consistency, clarity, and continuous improvement. Embracing a sales process as a habit ensures better results and impactful customer interactions.

What is a sales process?

A sales process is a series of defined stages and repeatable steps guiding salespeople from lead to customer. Think of it as a map for a mountain climb, helping navigate from the base to the summit. Stages, activities, and verifiable outcomes are essential components. Common steps include prospecting, contact, qualification, needs assessment, presentation, proposal, handling objections, gaining commitment, and follow-up. A customer-focused process eliminates unproductive actions, adding momentum toward commitment. A good sales process is flexible, scalable, and aligns with CRM systems for effective tracking and progression. Understanding these elements ensures a successful climb up the sales mountain.

Steps of a typical sales process

A well-defined sales process is more than just closing a deal; it guides the customer's journey from prospecting to post-purchase. It fosters lasting relationships, increasing customer lifetime value and reducing acquisition costs. The key steps include prospecting, making a good first impression, qualifying leads, conducting effective customer conversations, seamless onboarding, and post-purchase follow-up. Customizing these steps to fit your business needs ensures a successful sales process, acting as a map to guide prospects from initiation to the sales summit.

What is a sales methodology?

Your sales process is the map guiding prospects from start to finish, while your sales methodology provides the skills and techniques for effective navigation. Both are crucial, working in tandem for maximum impact. Sales methodologies, like the topology on a map, help navigate through stages with intentionality. They empower salespeople with proven approaches based on buying principles and field-tested tactics. For instance, an inbound sales methodology attracts prospects, and customer conversation methodology guides the story from opening to commitment. These methodologies are actionable how-to guides aligning with prospect and buyer needs throughout the sales cycle. Effective implementation requires organization-wide adoption, efficient training, and scalable coaching to build and refine sales skills. In essence, having a great map is essential, but being a skilled navigator at each stage is equally crucial for reaching the sales summit consistently.

How to leverage your methodology

In my view, the most crucial part of any sales methodology is the approach used in customer conversations. Your mindset matters; a service-oriented approach trumps a selling mindset. In the neuro selling customer conversation model, start by establishing a genuine connection and building personal trust. Share a personal connection story to set a positive tone. Then, introduce the prospect story to demonstrate understanding of their goals. Present the problem story, using third-party insights to highlight obstacles hindering the prospect's goals. Quantify the cost of not solving these problems. Transition to your product or solution story, showcasing differentiation and aligning your solution with previously discussed problems. Compare the solution's price to the problem's cost to illustrate real value. Identify and remove barriers to change, leading to a commitment. Mastering this methodology yields immediate benefits in sales and customer satisfaction.

Understand your buyer

Often, organizations design their sales process without considering the buyer's perspective, focusing too much on showcasing their company's features. It's crucial to develop a sales process with the buyer in mind, aligning it with their journey and needs. Just as car manufacturers tailor features to consumer demands, your sales process should adapt to what buyers seek. Understanding the buyer's journey, including pre-call planning, social media presence, and providing useful information during prospecting, is essential. Recognizing that buyers may not initially realize they need your product is part of effective prospecting. The evaluation stage requires establishing a connection, sharing insights, and demonstrating how your solution addresses their needs. The sales process extends beyond the sale, addressing buyer concerns and encouraging referrals. By focusing on the buyer's journey, your sales process becomes more natural, leading to increased sales and buyer satisfaction.

Document your sales process

While having a great sales process is beneficial, documenting it is crucial for accountability and efficiency. Follow these five key steps to effectively document your process:

1. Define the buying process from the buyer's perspective, outlining their steps from problem recognition to contract execution.

2. Fill in supporting details by putting yourself in the prospect's shoes and answering key questions at each stage.

3. Identify actions at each stage to help the prospect move forward based on their needs.

4. Determine how to measure progress, creating reporting requirements for the organization.

5. Estimate conversion rates at each stage to track progress, identify bottlenecks, and project revenue accurately.

This documentation enhances tracking, identifies issues, and ultimately leads to increased sales.

Define prospect flow

In the digital era, organizations often use tools like Salesforce, HubSpot, PipeDrive, or Copper CRM to manage their sales process. Regardless of the tool, defining how prospects flow through the process is crucial. Whether using digital platforms or Excel spreadsheets, it's vital to clearly outline each stage and criteria for progression. For instance, starting with the prospecting stage, contacts move through attempted contact, made contact, qualifying, sales meeting, and deal won or lost stages. Naming conventions can vary, but understanding each stage and its criteria ensures efficient prospect progression from initial contact to becoming a new customer.

Define metrics for success

Once you've defined your sales process steps, it's crucial to measure success at each stage to identify bottlenecks and optimize performance. In the prospecting stage, track the total number of prospects and the percentage that qualifies. For connecting or making initial contact, map out quality engagements and determine how many qualify for the next stage. In the qualifying stage, measure the number of leads fitting your qualification standards and those moving on to formal meetings. For the sales meeting stage, track live meetings and consider the average sales cycle. In onboarding, measure the time to get new customers up and running quickly. In follow-up or customer service, establish metrics for proactive check-ins, feedback requests, and referrals. Keep metrics simple for clarity and alignment across the organization, ensuring everyone understands the pipeline, revenue potential, and the path to creating satisfied customers.

What you should know, do, say, and show

The crucial part of a great sales process is the "moments of impact customer conversation" during the sales meeting or customer conversation (step four in our model). This step is the linchpin, and success hinges on how well it's executed. To excel in this phase, you should thoroughly research the prospect's goals, challenges, and business operations. Utilize a clear conversation roadmap that builds personal trust through connection and leverages storytelling focused on the prospect's agenda. Engage in visual storytelling, whether in-person or virtually, and use insightful questions to involve the prospect in the narrative. The key is to ensure that the prospect feels a sense of ownership in the solution you provide. Following these tips will enhance your readiness and contribute to a more positive experience for the prospect, ultimately leading to better outcomes for you.

Chapter 7 Sales Operations

What are sales operations?

Creating an exceptional sales organization involves more than just having great people and leadership. An often-overlooked aspect is the sales operations team, crucial for managing various non-quota aspects, aligning missions, and executing go-to-market strategies. The sales operations leader serves as a Chief Operating Officer, sales strategy partner, chief of staff, and a salesperson. Their role is multifaceted, requiring strong quantitative skills, strategic understanding, and effective collaboration. Hiring for sales operations involves seeking individuals with competencies in analytics, communication, strategic analysis, and collaboration, ideally with relevant industry experience. Building a successful sales organization hinge on the foundation provided by a proficient sales operations team.

Define and size your addressable market

Picture this: You're at your desk, and the sales head urgently instructs you to assign accounts to everyone. If you're like most, you're left wondering, "How do I build sales territories?" Territory planning involves logically dividing a market into manageable sections. The first step is defining and sizing your addressable market, understanding your target users and the value proposition of your product to them. This leads to determining your Total Addressable Market (TAM), calculated as addressable users multiplied by the average selling price per unit. Realistically defining your target users is crucial to avoid diluting sales resources. Starting with TAM helps gauge the market opportunity and allocate appropriate resources.

Develop a go-to-market strategy

When determining how to allocate go-to-market resources, companies often consider a combination of geography, market segment, and industry. Geographic considerations may include office locations, language capabilities, and culturally relevant assets for multi-country businesses. Industry sector specialization may be crucial for navigating unique regulatory environments or requiring specific technical knowledge, as seen in healthcare markets. Another crucial aspect is customer size or market segment, often categorized as Small/Medium Business (SMB), mid-market, and enterprise, each requiring distinct approaches based on company attributes and needs. Additionally, aligning efforts for existing and net new customers is crucial, as the skill sets for acquiring new customers differ from those needed to grow an existing customer base. Consider these dimensions—geography, industry, customer size—when developing a go-to-market strategy that optimizes resources for the opportunity at hand.

How to set up equitable sales territories

Creating fair and equitable sales territories is a crucial aspect of sales operations. Despite efforts to make territories fair, there may always be someone on the sales team who isn't satisfied, so aim to do your best. After determining your Total Addressable Market (TAM) and go-to-market strategy, the next step is to establish fair sales territories. The goal is to design territories where a sales rep given the chance to choose would find it challenging to identify a clear outlier in terms of attractiveness. This process is simpler in Small/Medium Business (SMB) territories, where a more mathematical approach can be applied. As you move up-market, judgment from the sales operations and leadership team becomes more critical. Tradeoffs include account size versus volume, distribution of account quality, logical geographic divisions, and considerations for named accounts. The process involves the sales ops team creating a data-driven first pass of territories, followed by a collaborative fine-tuning process with sales leadership to incorporate market-specific dynamics. Transparency, a clear decision-making framework, and frequent communication between sales operations and leadership are essential.

It's recommended to avoid giving the best accounts only to the top-performing reps to maintain a level playing field and facilitate accurate data analysis. Since market dynamics change, an annual territory planning process is advisable, unless the business is very young. Despite potential dissatisfaction, well-planned sales territories can significantly impact the success of the sales team.

How to set sales quotas

A quota is a fixed target, often monetary, set over a specific period, usually a year or less. It can also include targets like acquiring new customers or completing certain activities. Quotas drive salespeople through positive incentives for achieving and negative consequences for failing to reach them. There are two main types: direct quotas, assigned individually to sales reps, and overlay quotas, which sum up direct quotas. Overlay quotas extend to managers, VPs, and specialists aligned with specific products or services. Over assigning quotas, exceeding the company goal, is a best practice but requires balance. Quotas should be set based on the total addressable market (TAM) and need to be objective, attainable, and aligned with financial plans. Direct quotas can be categorized into new business and existing customer quotas. For new business, historical average selling prices and conversion rates help determine a realistic quota. Existing customer quotas consider expected revenue from renewals and incremental sales during the period. The process of setting quotas is a critical responsibility of the sales operations team, linking market sizing with sales compensation.

Incentive compensation: Variable pay

For newcomers, I suggest consulting with an experienced professional for a market analysis and recommended payout strategies. To create an effective sales compensation plan, focus on three elements: quotas, variable pay, and accelerators. Quotas represent target amounts for salespeople during the compensation period. Variable pay, comprising base salary and additional earnings based on performance against quota, is often termed On-Target Earnings (OTE). Use market data to determine competitive pay structures, including the pay mix between base and variable pay. Understand average quota achievement and other relevant metrics to ensure your compensation plan aligns with industry standards. While market data is a guideline, tailor your plan to best suit your company's needs.

Incentive compensation: Accelerators

To create an effective incentive compensation plan, focus on three components: reps' quotas, variable pay, and accelerators. Payout percentage is determined by dividing the quota by variable pay, usually with a slope for higher payouts at higher quotas. Accelerators come into play after hitting On-Target Earnings (OTE), motivating reps with higher payouts beyond OTE. Set accelerators based on an excellence point, a multiplier of both quota and variable pay, rewarding reps for exceeding performance expectations. Accurate quotas are crucial to avoid costly overpayments. Consider whether to include payout caps, balancing incentives with potential risks. Before constructing your sales comp plan, ensure clear definitions for quotas, variable pay, and accelerators.

Designing compensation plans

To create a comp plan, start by understanding market data and gathering input from impacted teams, including sales comp admin, sales leadership, finance, HR, and reps. Recognize that modern sales plans aim to incentivize and retain talent. Prioritize simplicity, avoiding complex metrics, and consider ease of administration. Connect payouts to contract signings or other factors like revenue to reduce payment risks. Emphasize a key metric if necessary, keeping the plan straightforward. Establish an exception process and communicate it clearly. Optionally, incorporate recognition-based incentives like a "club" for top performers. Ensure communication is led by sales leadership, and address ongoing mid-year contests (SPIFs) as secondary to the overall compensation plan. A well-designed and communicated incentive compensation plan aligns sales reps' interests with company goals, motivating and empowering the sales organization.

How forecasting works

Forecasting is a crucial function of sales operations, providing insights for business leaders and aiding in planning. A sales forecast is a financial model predicting the revenue a sales team will generate over time. To create an accurate forecast, you need to know the opportunity amount, close date, and forecast probability for each deal. There are two main forecasting methodologies: the bottoms-up approach, led by sales reps and managers, and the top-down approach, managed by the sales operations team. The bottoms-up approach involves summing individual forecasts, adjusting by managers, and capturing the difference as a buffer. In contrast, the top-down model relies on historical trends and pacing to predict outcomes. Combining both approaches yields a comprehensive view, enabling the identification of trends and factors affecting forecast performance. Mastering forecasting is essential for building a successful sales team within your sales operation's organization.

How to forecast

To establish your forecasting function, focus on acquiring the right tools and implementing a well-defined process. For the bottoms-up approach, where the sales team drives forecasting, set a regular meeting cadence, with teams providing forecasts weekly or biweekly. These forecasts should be tracked closely, and sales operations should run the meetings, circulating insights regularly. CRM tools like Salesforce.com and Microsoft Dynamics are essential for this approach, helping identify annualized business outlooks and tying forecast percentages to sales stages. For the top-down approach, which involves constructing a model based on historical trend analysis, strong quantitative skills are necessary. Build tools and processes for a data-driven approach to understand how your business will perform. Maintain data hygiene by centralizing data sources, ensuring consistency. Creating a culture of accurate forecasting is vital for a successful sales operation's organization.

Sales tools for your sales team

In the realm of operations, building a successful sales team requires not just excellent people and processes, but also the right technology. Sales operations play a crucial role in implementing, administering, and enhancing sales-related systems. Prioritizing projects and translating business requirements are guided by SOPs. The primary technology is the CRM system, which is central to scaling, enhancing productivity, and facilitating reporting.

Technology falls into three broad categories. Firstly, the "system of engagement" includes tools for day-to-day sales activities, encompassing outreach, marketing and sales automation, meeting tools, and sales intelligence tools. Integration with the CRM is essential for seamless data exchange.

Secondly, the "system of record" serves as the repository for account data and tracks key sales metrics and activities. It is critical for forecasting and operational reporting. Considerations for data quality, including deduping technology and a dedicated team, are emphasized for maintaining clean and reliable data.

Lastly, the "system of reporting" comprises databases and business intelligence tools integrated into either the system of record or other systems. This area is vital for generating reports and insights crucial for sales leadership and operations teams. A well-implemented set of sales technology systems can significantly enhance sales team performance, leading to increased revenue and cost savings for the business.

Invest in sales learning

Every organization requires a sales learning team to cultivate expertise in selling skills, product knowledge, and company business requirements. Sales training programs are essential to equip representatives with the information necessary for effective selling. However, many training programs fall short, focusing only on product understanding and go-to-market strategy. Despite skepticism from leaders and low ratings from sales reps, sales learning programs are crucial because sales involve more than just information—it requires understanding customer problems, mapping solutions, asking the right questions, and mastering persuasive techniques. Excelling in sales demands genuine effort, skills development, and an investment in improvement. Sales learning is challenging, with limited non-work time for adult learning.

Achieving success in sales learning requires support from leadership and commitment from participants. Adhering to the 70-20-10 rule of learning, where 10% comes from actual training, 20% from practice, and 70% from on-the-job training, is crucial. Sales learning should be treated as a mandatory job requirement. The core of any sales learning program is the sales methodology, outlining the sales team's philosophy, process, and best practices. Roles on a sales learning team include sales trainers collaborating with leadership, instructional designers creating content, and operations analysts measuring impact and suggesting improvements. Sales training is not optional; every sales team needs a sales training organization, and outstanding teams invest in creating a robust sales learning function.

How to build a world-class sales learning function

There are four developmental phases from good to great. The first is ad hoc training, which most businesses currently employ. It involves measurable training, whether in person or through e-learning, with a focus on assessing and retaining skills. The second phase is continuous learning, where an overarching curriculum guides the entire organization through an organized sales education journey. The third phase emphasizes scale and efficiency, leveraging technology to distribute content cost-effectively and measuring impact. Efficiency metrics such as cost per rep and curriculum development time become crucial. The fourth and final stage is personalized learning, utilizing data to micro-target skills based on individual needs. Striving for an outstanding sales learning function can significantly enhance sales team productivity.

Using data to sell

Data is more than a trend; it's a core methodology for making quality business decisions. In sales, data analytics serves two main purposes: internally, it helps analyze and prioritize customers based on value, and externally, it provides irrefutable evidence to support value assertions made to customers. Trust in data sources and methodologies is crucial, and understanding how customers measure value is key. Finding scalable ways to measure value against benchmarks or comparative companies is the final step.

Rules of engagement and account ownership

As a salesperson checking your morning email, you might encounter a situation where a peer closes a deal on an account that could be yours. This common occurrence highlights the need for Sales Operations to manage credit allocation through a process known as Rules of Engagement (ROE). ROE defines the crediting philosophy, addressing collaboration, sales coverage, territory ownership, and merit-based rewards. It clarifies account ownership for each sales rep, specifying rules for account holds and transfers, crucial in global account scenarios. The crediting philosophy should be designed for clarity, avoiding complications and unnecessary expenses, ensuring a fair and transparent system for sales credit.

Key components of the rules of engagement

The Rules of Engagement (ROE) are crucial for establishing sales processes and determining credit allocation. In the context of modern sales teams, "bookings" are a flexible measure of sales performance, unlike the specific accounting term "revenue." ROE components include considerations for splits, determining when they occur, and their impact on different organizational levels. Addressing unanticipated events, such as quota adjustments for mergers or acquisitions, is another key aspect. The ROE also outlines sales policies on pricing, discounting, account maintenance, and other critical areas. Building a comprehensive and flexible ROE helps manage disputes, sets behavioral expectations for reps, and provides essential operational guidance for successful selling within established rules.

Chapter 8 Communication within Teams

Establish roles

Regardless of whether your team is new or has worked together for years, there's always room to enhance communication and collaboration. Clearly assigning roles like meeting convener, recorder, and monitor can improve coordination, prevent duplication, and capitalize on opportunities. The convener, often the team leader, oversees meeting logistics, from deciding its necessity to scheduling. The recorder documents discussions, participants, and next steps, sharing minutes promptly. A monitor keeps discussions on track and within time limits, especially crucial in virtual meetings. These roles can be fixed or rotated, but their definition ensures focused and meaningful team meetings. If your team lacks assigned roles, consider incorporating this into your next meeting agenda.

Delegate responsibilities

Ensure effective team coordination by utilizing a RACI matrix—a tool that clarifies responsibilities. RACI stands for Responsible, Accountable, Consulted, and Informed. This matrix improves efficiency, reduces redundancies, and coordinates efforts within the team. Specify Responsible (task doer), Accountable (management authority), Consulted (advisory role), and Informed (awareness) for each team member. This approach establishes clear processes for smooth collaboration and ensures everyone is aligned on their roles and responsibilities as you work towards your goals.

RACI Matrix for Team Members and Actions:

	Responsible	Accountable	Consulted	Informed
Team Member 1	X		X	X
Team Member 2		X	X	X
Team Member 3	X			X

List of Actions:

1. Action A

2. Action B

3. Action C

4. Action D

5. Action E

6. Action F

7. Action G

Collaborate to establish team goals and charter

To foster effective teamwork, ensure alignment on goals, purpose, and collaboration processes. Define the purpose of your team, select appropriate goal-setting frameworks like KPIs or SMART goals, and establish shared objectives. Clarify conditions of satisfaction, outlining minimal requirements for project completion. Develop a team charter detailing collaboration commitment, including meeting ground rules, communication norms, decision-making processes, consequences for unmet expectations, and conflict resolution plans. Utilize a team charter template for guidance. Assign communication roles, align goals, and set conditions of satisfaction to ensure cohesive teamwork.

Team Charter

Team: [Team Name]

Date: [Date]

Charter Version: [Version]

Members:

- [Member 1 Name and Area]

- [Member 2 Name and Area]

- [Member 3 Name and Area]

Meeting Roles and Responsibilities

Purpose:

- Why has this team convened?

- What is your objective?

Conditions of Satisfaction

Commitments:

- What commitments are you making to each other?

Decision-Making:

- How will you make decisions?

Conflict:

- What will you do when conflict arises?

Information-Sharing Norms

- Name and Preferred Contact Info

General Ground Rules:

- Specifics about how and how often/when you will contact each other

Define expectations in your team

Teams with common goals may approach projects differently, emphasizing the need for clear documentation of expectations and norms. For instance, varying work styles between individuals like Ted and Fred can lead to friction if not addressed. Constructive conversations and a team charter outlining communication norms, operating procedures, and expectations can prevent conflicts. A newly-formed team's example demonstrates the importance of clarifying expectations during the charter development process. Team members should discuss and document details such as deadlines, meeting punctuality, and communication methods to avoid misunderstandings and ensure alignment.

Build trust in your team

Trust is crucial within teams, fostering collaboration and effective work. Teammates must rely on each other to fulfill commitments, attend meetings, and complete tasks as expected. Maintaining credibility is like filling a jar with coins—fulfilling promises adds coins, while missed commitments empty the jar, creating a challenge to rebuild. Eliminate the "say-do gap" by aligning words with actions. Trust also involves respecting teammates' intentions, avoiding negative behavior, and creating a culture of psychological safety where diverse perspectives can thrive. Additionally, competence is vital—teammates need to trust each other's ability to get the work done. Building and maintaining trust requires consistent effort, as it is fragile and can be quickly diminished. A team is a group of people who trust each other, emphasizing the importance of investing time in building strong team relationships.

Manage accountability within teams

Addressing accountability within a team is crucial to prevent recurring issues. Documenting expectations through the five W's—What needs to be done, When is the deadline, Who is responsible, Why is the task important, and What are the consequences—clarifies roles and promotes clarity. Discussing these details in meetings ensures everyone is on the same page. Confirming the five W's, as demonstrated by Carrie in the example, helps streamline communication and sets expectations for accountability. Teams should agree on consequences for meeting or failing to meet expectations, fostering a culture of shared wins and learning from mistakes without blame. Remember to document expectations to promote team accountability.

Provide feedback within teams

Actionable feedback is crucial for team success, but it can be challenging to give and receive. Establishing a feedback culture involves regularly sharing both positive and constructive feedback. The SBI framework—Situation, Behavior, Impact—provides a simple structure. Start with the specific Situation, detailing the exact moment in time. Describe the Behavior using verbs and focus on actions, not motives. Lastly, highlight the Impact on you or the team. An example in action involves addressing a missed deadline. The recipient's response should be a polite acknowledgment, even if there's disagreement. Avoid making excuses or getting defensive, treating feedback as a valuable gift. SBI works for positive feedback as well, making it a natural and beneficial practice for teams.

Manage conflict within teams

Conflict on teams is inevitable, and when managed productively, it can lead to positive outcomes. Two common sources of conflict are task and interpersonal.

Task conflict arises from disagreements on how work is done or the process for delivering results. Diverse teams may experience task conflict due to varying perspectives. Interpersonal conflict involves differences in values, personality, needs, and preferences. Identifying the type of conflict is crucial for resolution. Effective communication strategies can mitigate conflict. Acknowledge the issue, find a suitable time for discussion, establish ground rules, and provide equal time for each person to articulate their perspective. Use non-judgmental language, focusing on observable behavior. Encourage understanding, not necessarily agreement. Teammates then decide how to proceed, whether to end the discussion or continue. Reflect on the conflict to avoid future issues, emphasizing the importance of a well-developed team charter for reducing misunderstandings and conflicts.

Communicating virtually within teams

Virtual teams present both advantages and challenges, and improving their performance hinges on effective communication. Building connections with colleagues is crucial, achieved through virtual spaces for conversations, regular social events, and asking open-ended questions to encourage sharing. Use appropriate technology for work-related communication, considering the nature of the information and the likely response of the recipient. Documentation is key, and using a centralized method accessible to the entire team ensures everyone stays informed about work status and next steps. Optimal team communication, even in dispersed global teams, contributes to improved performance.

Cross-cultural communication within teams

Global teams benefit from diverse perspectives, but cross-cultural communication poses challenges. The LESCANT model—Language, Environment, Social organization, Context, Authority, Non-verbal, and Time—helps address these issues. In language, prioritize clear and basic phrasing to avoid misunderstandings, considering potential differences in fluency. Evaluate external cultural factors affecting the team's dynamics in the environment category. Social organization involves understanding how religion, race, gender, and class impact team dynamics. Context considers high or low-context communication cultures, emphasizing explicitness or implicitness. Authority examines cultural perspectives on leadership and hierarchies. Nonverbal communication, or body language, should be observed to ensure everyone's participation. Lastly, time perceptions can vary; some view it as flexible, while others adhere strictly to schedules. Discussing these factors and linking them to the team charter enhances cross-cultural communication and strengthens the team.

Measure success within teams

Regularly evaluating your team's progress is vital for long-term success. Conduct an After Action Review (AAR) at key project milestones or completion. This simple yet powerful process involves a team meeting with ground rules: involve everyone, encourage honest discussion, dismantle hierarchies, and establish a positive environment. Ask key questions in the AAR, such as: What was supposed to happen? What did happen? What worked well and why? What needs to change and why? How can we improve our process going forward? Engage the entire team, encourage open communication, and focus on learning from both successes and failures to foster continuous team growth.

After-Action Review Team: _____

Date: _____

Midstream [ ]

Project Completed: [ ]

Review Questions:

1. What was expected to occur?

2. Successful Aspects:

   - Why did they work well?

3. Areas for Improvement:

   - Lessons learned from the experience.

   - Process enhancements for the future.

Key Insights: _____

The imperative of effective teams

Improving collaboration and teamwork skills can transform your career, as most teams fall short of their potential. This book provides techniques to help you contribute effectively to team goals, addressing challenges in interpersonal communication, collaboration, and the phenomenon of social loafing. Whether you're concerned about unequal work distribution or damaging relationships, implementing best practices in team communication can counteract these issues. Refer back to this content for a refresher when facing challenges or joining new teams.